Dollars & No Sense

- Why Are You Spending Money Like An Idiot?

By: Simeon Lindstrom

Dollars & No Sense
– *Why Are You Spending Money Like An Idiot?*

Let's kick off this book with a simple question: what is money?

It's not a rhetorical question. Find a pen and paper and jot down a few sentences explaining what *you* think money is. Imagine aliens landed on your lawn and demanded a quick explanation for this strange phenomenon called money. What would you tell them?

Seems simple, but try it and you'll soon realize that it's tricky to answer. Money is many different things to people.

What is it to you?

In this book, we'll be tackling the familiar challenges of personal finance management ... but in an unfamiliar way. In the chapters that follow, we'll consider that money is whatever you make of it; it's pure potential and possibility, something you can yourself define and use to your own ends.

If your main money problem is simply "I don't have enough of it!" you may be surprised at the approach we take below. Here, you won't find the same old tips and tricks on how to save money by re-using teabags or buying rice in bulk. Instead, we'll get to the very heart of what money actually *means*, how we spend it and why, and what you can do to start using what you have right now to create a lifestyle that has meaning for you.

We'll consider the root causes of careless spending, as well as the three biggest but largely invisible money myths we all believe in to some extent. We'll then consider ways to start creating a budget that works *for* you and your goals, rather than against it.

Ready?

Spending Like Crazy – Signs That Your Money Habits Need Therapy

Have you ever opened your wallet and thought, hey where did all my money go?

Have you ever seen someone who ostensibly earns less money than you yet somehow they seem to have a much nicer lifestyle?

Do you ever get the creeping sensation that you're just a rat in a wheel, and that you're never really *getting anywhere* when it comes to money?

Are you often obsessed with buying something and then immediately lose interest in it the second you own it?

Do you feel like you have so much "stuff" but that you don't really need or even like most of it?

Do you ever sit at work and think, "what's the point of all this?!"

Does it seem like you spend a lot of your day stressing about money instead of just living?

Do you feel like you're moving from one minor money crisis to the next?

Are you in massive debt and feel sick to the stomach just thinking about how much you owe?

Are you often in relationships, jobs or living situations that you hate simply because you can't afford to try anything else?

If any of the above hit a little too close to home, then this book was written for you. Our culture has a strange blind spot when it comes to money – we'll watch ads for erectile dysfunction medicine on TV without flinching, overshare about our bowel movements and mother issues on social media, but when it comes to a frank discussion about money, many of us are more than a little shy. Money is a leading cause of relationship dissatisfaction, of stress and burnout, and yet we're all super reluctant about bringing it up. You're not supposed to talk about how much you earn. Or how much you *owe*, for that matter.

The result? Many of us have pretty dysfunctional relationships when it comes to money. Even the most put-together person can have an attitude to money that's a little bonkers. Read the following descriptions and see if any of them (or all of them!) sound like you.

The manic depressive spender:

The few days just before payday feel like Christmas Eve to you. You wait and anticipate, and the second you see your new bank balance, you're spending like there's no tomorrow, "treating" yourself to every little thing you know you deserve, spoiling your friends and enjoying the finer things in life. But by the time mid-month comes rolling by, you've overspent and have a horrible money hangover – and have to endure a miserable few weeks where you scrape by, borrow or live on beans and humiliation. But it's ok because your next payday is coming!

The money addict:

You're probably wealthier now than you've ever been, yet somehow life's expenses have just racked up at the same pace, and your sense of always slightly struggling seems to be the only constant. If money was a drug, well, you developed a tolerance for it a long time ago. What a younger version of yourself would have thought of as success and luxury barely registers at all for you anymore. You're pretty sure there's only one thing that would puncture your thickening skin of boredom and entitlement: more money...

The denial case:

Money is the root of all evil. And it also makes the world go round? Or something. You don't pay too much attention to your credit card statements and you plan on dying young anyway so you never have to stress too much about a pension. You've never been "good with money," you tell yourself, and the only thing you know for sure is that there's always somehow never enough of it. Financial planning and saving sound like things other people do. Things always work out, right? Until they don't. The more irresponsible you are with your finances, the deeper you stick your head into the sand...

Of course, these descriptions are just tongue-in-cheek – poor spending habits and unhealthy attitudes to money can seriously undermine your happiness and wellbeing and are no laughing matter. Money is a resource. It's a symbol. A tool. The way you think about yourself, your life and your worth is keenly reflected in the way you think about money. But in the next chapter, we'll see that most of us don't take money nearly as seriously as we should...

Why Normal Budgeting Advice Seldom Works

So, knowing all of the above, you might decide that you need some expert advice. After all, the next biggest section at the bookstore after self help ...is personal finance. People grinning like politicians grace the covers of these books, promising that if only you'd just sit down and organize yourself properly, you can get your life together, like them.

So you force yourself to read through these pep-talks, feeling sheepish to discover that you don't really understand compound interest after all, and that at the rate you're going, you can probably only think about retiring at about 95. Depressing!

Let's say you push through and do actually learn a few new tips and tricks to hack yourself into financial shape. Even though you keep it up for a while, your real life is never quite reflected in those pages. People on online personal finance forums tell you to register a business in the Cayman Islands so you can avoid tax, or to keep a piggy bank by your front door so you can save a bit here and there. It's not like these are *bad* ideas, but it's just that somehow... it doesn't seem to fit your life. Why?

Most budgeting advice likes to pretend that poverty is never really an issue.

There are lots of reasons your standard personal finance advice never quite "sticks." Let's get the most awkward and uncomfortable one out in the open first, the big elephant in the room that many of the above finance books will just conveniently pretend doesn't exist.

Call it poverty, "struggling", hardship or just plain old not having quite as much money as you need or want, it all amounts to the same thing. And in the same way that a book about dieting macros isn't much help to someone struggling to feed themselves at all, lofty personal finance philosophies that teach you what kind of property you'd best invest in first are ...a bit of a slap in the face.

An acquaintance once told me at a party, "Honestly at our age, if you're not saving at least X each month, you're crazy." The X he was alluding to was astronomically high to me; more, in fact, than many people in my area even made in a month – myself included. The shame and panic I felt then is characteristic of so much financial advice out there. Instead of helping people solve the real lifestyle issues they actually face in life, it makes hurtful assumptions. Pair this with the fact that most people are socialized to never talk about money, to never admit it if they're not doing too well, and you get a nasty cocktail of secrecy and shame around money, instead of realistic ways to tackle problems.

Most budgeting advice fails to take YOU into account.

This is really an extension of the above. Most budgeting advice out there assumes you're living a Standard American Life with all the trimmings, are in relatively stable employment, have a spouse and live with the unspoken assumption that you'll want a pension plan and an Xbox and a house for your 2.4 children.

The funny thing about this weird dream is how few people *actually* live it. We've all somehow agreed that this is the way it should be, or the way we want it to be, all the while living lives that are completely different. People are marrying less and cohabiting more, switching careers more, working many part time jobs instead of a single full time one, working from home, or doing strange blends of all of the above. People are leaving home ...then moving back in with their parents. Property has never cost so much for most of the developed world. People spend more on electronics and holidays now, less on cars, furniture, or raising children.

If you're a single parent, a mature student with two part-time jobs, struggling after a divorce or sharing a mortgage with your three sisters, most budgeting advice out there is going to look like a 1950s fairytale to you – nice, but not exactly realistic.

Most budgeting advice is value-neutral.

This is not exactly true. Most advice you'll stumble on *is* actually built on a series of beliefs the author will assume you share with them. It's just that these assumptions are so entrenched it's hard to even notice they're there. We all instinctively know that money is a

Big Deal, but perhaps because it's such an emotional and touchy subject for so many of us, we like to keep our distance and treat money literacy the same we treat household maintenance or yearly dental checkups.

But money is right at the heart of the way we live our lives. It's part of our identities, part of how we se ourselves and our achievements, part of how we construct meaning for ourselves and others. It's as personal as religion or sexual orientation. It's not value neutral. It's possible to learn to deal with money on a surface level – but unless you look a little deeper and explore what money actually means to you, you'll be missing what makes money such a big deal in the first place. Money is a proxy for *value*. It's human shorthand for all the things we've decided are worth something. And because of this, no discussion about money is complete without a discussion about value – specifically *our values*.

Tapping into Your Money Psychology

All well and good, but so what? What does that mean for you, someone who wants to learn healthier spending habits and take charge of their financial life?

Well, the advice in this book will try buck the trend and offer money advice from a completely different perspective. If you want to learn more about your 401k or what schemes are available for first time home owners, that information is easily available to you. If you need to understand how to pay down your credit card more effectively or what to do with your student loans, then rest assured you'll find answers at your local bank, or online, or by asking your accountant (if you have one!).

This book will simply not cover these issues – or at least, not directly.

Instead, we'll take a step back and ask ourselves *why*. Why do some people rack up huge amounts of debt and others don't? Why do some people make so much but seem to spend it all, while others earn half what they do and seem twice as happy? Why do people buy things the way they do? Why are some people petrified to open their credit card statements while some trade forex "for fun"?

These are not just idle questions though: once you truly understand *why* and *how* you think about money, then you can actually start to make lasting, realistic changes to the way you make, spend and save it.

If you read through the first chapter of this book and found yourself nodding in agreement, chances are you're guilty of a few "money misconceptions." These are myths about money that we've all either been taught or have learnt from our life experiences – but which are nevertheless keeping us back. These unquestioned beliefs about money can keep us from taking an honest, realistic look at where were we really are in our financial lives ...and were we really want to be.

By the end of this book, my hope is that you have a clarified idea of what money *really* means to you, and its role in helping you live a life that aligns with your own principles. But before we can do that, let's have a look at some ideas that may be limiting you in your life right now. You'll get the opportunity to ask yourself, is this really what *I* believe? Is this idea helping my ultimate goals – or hindering them?

Three Big Money Myths – and Why They Don't Make Sense

Money Can Buy You Love:

If you've ever casually studied advertising, you'll know that this is one of the fundamental underlying principles. Somewhere along the line, companies realized that merely telling their prospective customers about the characteristics of their product was no good – what they needed to do was sell a lifestyle. In other words, promote the idea that money can buy you love.

And it can buy you every other wonderful emotion, too. When you see the toilet cleaner ad on TV, it's not advertising toilet cleaner, it's selling you the opportunity to be a good wife, to create a safe and hygienic environment for your children. People don't sell cars, they sell freedom. They don't advertise perfume by telling you that it smells like neroli and jasmine, but that it smells like *scantily clad Charlize Theron ascending a luxurious silk rope, pearls and jewels smashing to the floor beneath her.*

Though most of us pay lip service to the idea that money can't buy you love, our spending habits betray the fact that actually ...that's exactly what we're hoping for. In a capitalist society, everything is for sale. You don't only buy a product to do a particular job, you buy yourself, an image of you in the future, using that product, living the kind of life of someone who uses that product.

This is why so many advertisements show people and not the product they're selling. This is why Apple had such extraordinary success marketing themselves against the boring "PC guy" – their marketers understood keenly that their customers weren't only shopping for good laptops and phones, they were primarily *shopping for their own identities.*

Now all of this makes good sense if you're in the business of selling things to impressionable people. Marketing departments spend huge amounts of money to make sure they're digging deep into people's psyches and tweaking just the right strings to get them to buy. They make unspoken promises that spending money will make you more attractive, more sophisticated, more intelligent, more successful.

If you think you're immune to this kind of thing, think again. Advertising evolves as people become more aware – if you've ever paid a little extra for "artisanal" anything or happily bought a product because it promised it was fair trade, you've been had in just the same way. Marketers understand that modern man doesn't want to be manipulated and sold to – so they are careful to make products that people can buy and which show how alternative/progressive they are, how savvy and countercultural. How *un*manipulable they are! It's dirty business.

If you've bought into any of this, one obvious consequence is that you develop the habit of solving problems by *buying* things. Bored? Buy something entertaining. Feeling like life is meaningless? Buy something that makes you feel like you're important. Lonely? Buy some drinks. Get your nails done. Save for a car.

Trying to buy positive emotions doesn't make sense because, for the most part, it just doesn't work. If you buy some expensive high heels because they make you feel like you're finally an adult with a sophisticated grown-up, legitimate job – well, what happens when those shoes break or get dirty or go out of fashion? You never learn to develop your *own* inner sense of worth and confidence. You defer the lesson, you put the psychological work outside of yourself, and into a thing that is inevitably short lived and fleeting. In a few weeks your new shoes start to look just as boring as all your other shoes.

So you're flipping through a magazine one day and see a beautiful, young girl with dazzling ruby lips. Your brain thinks it's finally found a solution. You never needed those old shoes anyway, no, what you really need now is to buy this gorgeous lipstick. And the cycle continues. What never changes is who you are, inside. You never ask yourself, who am I? What does it mean to be an "adult"? What am I looking for? What am I proud of? What do I want to do in this world, today, right now? These nagging questions are soothed temporarily by the rush of something new and shiny – but they never go away. The people who invented the term "retail therapy" knew what they were talking about...

How to stop BUYING solutions to life's problems:

If you identify with this myth, well, you have your work cut out for you. Taking a moment to stop and truly think about your behavior takes a lot of effort. Spending carelessly, being drawn to endless new things but never satisfied, well, that's the default. That's the easy setting. Breaking out of this can be difficult. But it can be done!

To begin, get into the habit of asking yourself *why* before every purchase. No need to send yourself into a weird existential spiral about it, though. Just ask yourself, as honestly as possible, if you're trying to buy an emotion.

Are you trying to redeem your bad lifestyle choices and feel morally superior by buying some overpriced "health food"? Are you buying one brand of smartphone instead of the other because of its price and features, or because you're hoping unconsciously to be one of the "cool kids' by having that particular phone?

Of course, there's no law to say you can't do any of this ...only try to be aware. Once you're in the habit of seeing why you're *really* buying something (peer pressure, advertising) you'll loosen its grip on you. You'll also give yourself the opportunity to address your issues *directly*. If you're bored or sad or frustrated, pause before you jump in to buy a solution.

Is there another way to give yourself that feeling? A way that doesn't involve spending money?

Challenge: Sometime within the next week, challenge yourself to not buy something you were thinking of buying. Now, instead of consuming, see if you can turn things around and *produce* instead. Instead of going out for a fancy dinner, why not stay home, challenge yourself to make your own gourmet meal and invite your favorite person to enjoy it with you in a pillow fort in your living room? Instead of blowing money on a premium handcrafted children's bunk bed you saw on Pinterest, enjoy your children by taking them on an impromptu road trip or picnic where you paint watercolors for the afternoon, or take the opportunity to teach your children about woodwork and painting and build a bed yourself. Don't binge on chocolate when you're feeling down, call your mom. You get the idea!

Your Bank Balance = Your Life Report Card:

When you were in school, the custom was to give you a periodic report card to let your parents know that you were keeping up (officially) and how you rated compared to the other kids (unofficially). Though many parents and schools have abandoned the idea of ranking and scoring children in a learning environment this way, the fact is that this attitude is just as prevalent as ever. Most of us still cling to a vague sense of being measured and ranked according to our peers.

We approach our 30th or 40th birthdays, wondering whether our peers are ahead of us in just the same way our mothers stressed when we were the last ones to learn to spell, or when we didn't score high enough in our exams. From early on in life, we are told that human life, learning and progress can be quantified, and once it is, the name of the game is competition.

So, although most people who disagree that they think this way, we all secretly understand that the engineer who earns $200 000 a year is "worth" more than the teacher who earns $20 000. We encourage people to ask for raises by telling them, "you're *worth* it!"

But is this really true?

Far be it for me to downplay the achievements of the world's businessmen and entrepreneurs, and all those who have earned money from their ideas, talents and hard work. It would be strange to suggest that those who are skilled and work hard should not be rewarded.

But.

Thinking of your bank balance as your "life report card" is what is truly diminishing. It reduces a person's entire life achievements to a figure (or several figures), focusing only on those things that can be priced, quantified and put into a spread sheet. In other words, what can be bought or sold.

What you get when you look at the world this way is one-dimensional people. You get the super-successful CEO who sits alone in his expensive condo at night, feeling that for all his money, he's still strangely unfulfilled. You get stay at home parents who experience deep and profound feelings about the work they do, confident about their life's meaning right up to the point were someone dismisses them as "unemployed" and therefore worth exactly nothing.

When you view yourself as a being whose purpose is to make money, and the balance in your bank account as your "score," you rob yourself of a fuller experience of your life. You tick all the financial boxes and feel empty. You wonder what it's all for.

How to stop being defined by your salary:

Challenge: Make a "Life Resume." You don't have to literally write out a CV as you would when looking for a job, but give it some thought: what are your life's achievements? Not as a cog in a machine or as an employee in someone else's company, but as a human being.

What skills do you have? We often write off everything we are and know if it can't be sold on the job market. We forget that we are also husbands and wives, parents, friends, community members. Who we are is so much more than what we can sell ourselves for in the marketplace. Thinking of yourself as earning a score just leads you to ugly feelings of competition where you downplay all the things that make you unique – not to mention all the ways *other* people are unique too! Competition shuts you off from creative solutions. Ironically, it's the real visionaries and free-thinking entrepreneurs, the ones that follows their hearts, that end up making the most money and being more successful anyway!

I Did It All for the Money:

Go to any big-box homeware store in the suburbs and you will see a familiar sight: a busy woman dragging around her bored-to-death partner who can't fake any more enthusiasm for flower shaped candleholders or ceramic birds or beaded lampshades. "But what's this all *for*?" he whines to his girlfriend, who thinks of him as some kind of uncultured idiot.

He has a good point. What is it all for?

For our final "money misconception," lets look at all the ways that you might be tempted to treat money as a goal in and of itself, rather than a tool that helps you achieve your life goals. This is the difference between working for money, rather than money working for you, as cheesy as it sounds. It's a subtle difference, but it lies in the fact that money isn't actually a thing, it's a thing that allows you access to *other things*. What those other things are is entirely up to you. But surprisingly, many of us forfeit this question entirely.

We make enough money to get buy. We save because it's what we're told we should do. We pay the bills and get on with it. But unless you have a *plan* for the things you spend money on, then they're all just as useless as those homeware knick knacks the girl in our story wastes money on. Think about it.

If an item or service adds literally nothing to your life, it's basically the same as you taking that money and throwing it away. You may feel as though you've achieved something in merely earning it, but unless that money was actually put to use in helping you achieve your life's goals – what was it for? You have a lump of savings, which feels nice, but again, what's it for?

Most of us are told to just earn money – and the more the better. Keep getting promotions. Keep earning more. There's a dim understanding of what you'll eventually do with it (buy a house? Retire eventually?) but very few people actually sit down, look at what they earn and ask themselves, how am I going to *use* this?

It can be sobering to look at someone who earns less than what we do, living our dreams and carving out a lifestyle for themselves that we ourselves want. But if you never ask yourself the question (what do I want?) your money will come and it will go again ...and your dreams will languish, never actualized. You'll die and maybe leave a chunk of your life's earnings to the next generation, and your only legacy will be a material one – if that. Bleak, isn't it?

This misconception ties into the others, and is built on the idea that money by itself is enough, that money isn't a shorthand for value, but *is* value, not just a symbol for success, but all of what success is. That merely earning it and squirrelling it away is more or less the same thing as living life successfully. It's a rather elaborate way that we tell ourselves we can buy an emotion – in this case, the emotion is one of success, of completeness and accomplishments. When a rapper rolls around in a bath of cash in a music video, the implication is clear – the money *itself* is the achievement.

The trouble is, again, that this line of thinking just doesn't make any sense. Your unfulfilled goals and dreams are still there, nagging at you, your misconceptions remain unchallenged, and your values and principles remain untested. The sheer number of wealthy and yet personally undeveloped people in this world is proof enough that money is just a tool. And like any other tool, it can be used well, or it can sit there and do nothing useful.

How to remember that money is just a tool:

Maybe you can remember being a kid and thinking how when you grew up, you'd be in charge and could do and buy whatever you wanted. What happened to those dreams?

In the previous challenge, you tried to re-imagine a Life Resume that focused on all of your life's accomplishments and skills, not just those that can be labeled with a price tag. While you'll obviously need some marketable skills out there, the idea of this challenge was to remind you of your other dimensions, and that you are so much more than an employee or a tax payer.

In this challenge, we'll do something a little similar. Instead of looking at your budget and seeing only the cold, hard figures, draw up an alternative "Values Budget." In this budget, you won't merely be tallying up the actual money you have coming in and going out – you'll instead be tracking *how well you use that money,* however much it is.

If you're routinely squandering money on things you just don't care about, and which add nothing to your own sense of fulfillment, then you have a bad budget, and it doesn't matter how much you earn.

Sit down with a pen and paper and start brainstorming two or three of your ultimate life values.

These are the things that are important to you, the non negotiables of your life, the things, maybe, that you'd be prepared to die for. This is what gives you a sense of satisfaction and purpose at the end the day, or what guides each of your actions. Don't worry if you haven't worked out a crystal clear set of values for yourself, but ask yourself the question anyway.

Now, let's say you've narrowed it down to two very special life values that you believe are more important to you than anything else: the happiness of your family and the belief that you should always, no matter what, try to grow and expand your mind, and learn new things. Other possible values could include independence, artistic expression, romantic love, building something useful, fame or spiritual connection. It doesn't really matter.

Now, if you're like the average human being, you'll probably be using around a third of your total time sleeping or doing general "life admin" like eating, showering, getting dressed, walking from one place to another. That's around 8 hours. For argument's sake, let's say you're in full time employment and expected to work 8 hours a day. The remaining 8 hours are yours, let's say for recreation.

Though there's not much wiggle room when it comes to sleeping or "life admin," the rest of your day is up to you. Look at the relative proportions of time you spend on different activities and ask yourself if they match your principles and values. If you value your family's happiness and the ability to learn new things more than anything else – does your schedule actually reflect that?

Don't only look at how much time you're "spending" on certain activities, but also how much actual money. You may well re-consider your identity as a lifelong learner and family man if you only total $45 and 2.5 hours per month on both of these values. Look at what you *are* spending time and money on. Are these the things that deeply move you and give your life meaning?

You may discover a pretty obvious root cause of unhappiness: that your daily habits (including your money habits) don't truly align with your higher values. You may be wasting precious time working at a job you don't really care about only to spend all that money on things and activities you don't really care about either.

The great thing about an expanded budget such as this one is that it's *not* value neutral. Money has value in your life to the extent that you can use it for the things that make you happy and fulfilled. What does it matter to be frugal and pinch pennies if you have no real sense of what a saved penny can do for you anyway? What good is a raise or end-of-year bonus if it can only buy you *more* of the same things that don't really fulfill you?

- Decide on your values (pick two or three)
- Look at what you actually spend your time and money on – are your habits and values well-aligned?
- Can you take the time and money you spend on things that don't enrich you and funnel them towards things that do?

You could find novel ways to use coupons to buy budget cereal or buy a second hand appliance instead of a new one. But you reap greater rewards when you take a *full, comprehensive* look at your life and ask how money is and isn't serving you. With that in mind, let's move onto some real, practical ways to start improving your relationship with money, from the ground up.

Smart Ways to Think About Your Money

The only way to make meaningful changes in your life is to do something you haven't done before.

Begin with the attitude, "what if this wasn't the way it is, but some other way?"

Be willing to drop all the assumptions you make each and every day, and be open to new possibilities. Like any lifestyle change, revamping your attitude to money takes patience and the willingness to form new and healthier habits. As you complete the exercises listed here, as well as those that will follow, try to maintain a curious, open frame of mind:

Be aware, be in control:

You can't change what you're not aware of. Decide today that you'll take charge of money, rather than feeling like it is in charge of you. For people who've grown up in homes where money was scarce, the feeling that resources will always be scarce is hard to shake. But you are in control. You decide what thoughts you have, and the thoughts you have determine your behaviors and habits.

It may seem like a small thing at first, but often, the biggest transformations in life happen when we look honestly at our thoughts, feelings and behaviors and see them for what they are. You might have an out of control spending habit, one where you blow huge amounts of money every weekend on overpriced drinks. But one day you stop for a second, look at the drink in your hand and think, *is this really worth it*? And then you look closely at just how much money you waste every month this way, and you add it up over each year, over a lifetime. You think about how you've stupidly told your friends, "I'd love to study part time, I just can't afford it." You decide to change your lifestyle, to start spending money on the things you really value. It's hard work, but none of it would have started without that first thought, that first moment of awareness.

Have the courage to keep asking yourself, what am I doing now? Why am I doing this? Is this what I want? Am I happy? What if this wasn't the way it is now, but some other way?

Make the choice:

It's an old truism that if you don't choose, someone else will be happy to choose for you, and this is also true of all things money-related. If you don't negotiate for a higher salary, you'll get the default one. If you don't make an effort to make and stick to a budget, there will be millions of people out there who will happily take your money from you. If you don't actively choose where to spend your money, you may find that it somehow gets eaten up by the end of the month anyway.

Be proactive when it comes to your finances. Realize that money is nothing but *potential*. It can be whatever you want it to be: savings for a rainy day, a smaller investment into something big and important, a momentary bit of pleasure, security, a way to survive, something fun and ego-boosting ...anything. So use it wisely.

Don't focus on lack – be grateful instead:

It's easy to fall into the frame of mind where you're punishing yourself, where you're on a kind of diet where you're not allowed to spend or enjoy yourself. This may be the case for those "manic depressive spenders" we spoke about above. The problem with this kind of attitude is that you work against yourself, and set yourself up for failure. And you make overspending seem extra attractive!

If you feel miserable when moderating your spending, take some time to remind yourself that you're making active choices, and that you don't *have to*, rather you want to. Remind yourself of your values. Try not to focus on all the things you don't have, but be grateful for the things you do.

Many people recommend a "gratitude journal" and as cheesy as it sounds, it's a remarkably easy way to remind yourself of how fortunate you already are. Instead of becoming numb to all the wonderful things that are already in your life, take the time to remember how lucky you are to eat well, to have the luxuries you do, to have friends and family, or even for the blessing of sitting outside in a park with the warm sun on your face.

Try jotting down 10 things that you're grateful for every single day. This will not only unlock old wells of pleasure and life satisfaction you might have forgotten about, but it will keep you aligned with your higher values and principles.

Adapt and learn:

Things change ...and so should you. What works in your early twenties won't work in your retirement years. As your life circumstances change and develop, your attitude to money should be flexible enough to change along with it.

Have a five-year plan, but make it a flexible one, one that can grow and adapt as needed. As you make changes to your spending habits and money lifestyle, you may of course stumble on something that doesn't work. That's OK. Trial and error (emphasis on the error) is just part of learning.

Keep in mind that just because you did something once before, doesn't mean you have to keep doing it. You're allowed to change your mind. And you're allowed to be wrong. Think of it this way: you either succeed, or you learn. You only fail when you look at the outcomes of a lifestyle change and fail to take any lessons from it. So, feel free to read something in these pages, try it out for yourself and then decide that nope, it won't work for you.

Trim Your Budget – and Your Life

We've looked at three of the most common underlying money misconceptions that are probably getting in the way of a money lifestyle that truly serves you. We've looked at some of the hidden beliefs that may be quietly limiting your ability to use money for what it is: a tool that can help you achieve your goals and create a life that fits with your values and principles.

Let's take a more practical look at your actual budget now, but try to keep in mind this bigger picture. Below we're going to look at ways to bring your actual spending habits closer in line with what's important to you. We'll look at ways to take the insanity out of spending and get a greater sense of control and awareness over how you use your money. You can follow the outline suggested below as often as you like. And since money advice is only good advice if it actually works for your life, feel free to adapt and adjust it as necessary.

Step one - Take a good hard look:

If you haven't already, it's time to look at what you spend in a typical month. You'd be surprised how few people know exactly what they spend and where. In fact, if you're hesitant to even look properly, ask yourself if there's something you're trying to avoid looking at too closely.

You can appraise your monthly spending in a few ways: looking at bank statements and going through each item carefully, highlighting every expense according to the type (eating, entertainment, clothing, schooling, debt etc.) is an easy and obvious way to start. You might like to download a money management app that will allow you to look at your expenses in a variety of ways – sometimes graphs and pie graphs really drive the point home.

Look at what percentage of your total income you're spending on each area (i.e. 30% on rent, 10% on food), look at savings and if you can, try to identify any long term trends (i.e. your rent keeps going up but your salary is staying the same, or you keep going into debt every January after Christmas).

It's just data at this point so try to stay curious and pretend it's someone else's spending you're looking at. If something feels too scary or depressing to look at, that's your cue to look even closer at it...

Step two - Rate how well this budget is suiting your needs:

As we've seen, most money management advice out there has a very simplistic take on budgets: more money is good, less is bad. But I hope you've been convinced now to look at your budget with higher expectations.

Look at your spending habits in all their glory. Look at that awkward lump of debt you'd rather not think about. Look at your salary, what you (really!) spend on gym, on internet, on coffee and snacks, on medical expenses. Now, recall to mind your "life resume" and "values budget" from earlier chapters. Whether you did this exercise in full or merely thought about it, try to remember now what your ultimate values are as a human being, and what your achievements in life thus far have been.

Now, ask yourself, are your spending habits helping or hindering you in these values and achievements? Are you spending in alignment with these ideas – or in direct opposition to them?

Look for areas where you bleed a lot of money into things you don't actually care about. If you only buy a coffee and a snack every day at work because you're bored and unfulfilled, you're spending inefficiently. If you can identify where you are trying to "buy your emotions," then you can cut that spending and think of real ways to address that emotional need – you'll help yourself and save that cash all at the same time.

You may notice that wasting a hundred dollars each month on expensive coffee and treats during lunch hour is just a small thread – but pull on it and you may discover it leads to bigger lifestyle changes you might be ready for. You may discover that overspending in this area only happens because you're bored with your job and need to ask for more challenging projects. This may be just the impetus to admit that it's time to ask for a promotion or look for another job. Had you merely tried the standard budgeting advice (buy a coffee machine for home instead and take it work in a thermos! Have tea instead, it's cheaper!) you've gone a step further and made meaningful changes to your lifestyle.

Take a moment to look and see whether your spending habits and attitude to money is doing its job of helping you achieve your goals.

Step three - Re-prioritize:

If you're reading this book, the answer to the previous question may be "hell no." That's fine. Without changing your total income or your total expenditure, attempt now to reshuffle and put your resources to their *best* possible use. Is your lifelong goal of learning to play the violin more important than wasting hours every evening binge watching series? Then stop paying for TV each month and funnel that money instead into a fund for violin lessons. If you value the idea of making meaningful change in the world, or of doing the right thing, cut that useless gym membership you keep paying for and offer to volunteer at a dog shelter instead. You still get some exercise, you save money *and* you do something that's ultimately worth so much more to you.

Think creatively here. Don't assume you "need" something. Ask yourself honestly if you just *want* it. Some choices can be difficult of course, and most of us are working with very limited incomes. But make this easier for yourself by contextualizing: going to the movies every weekend feels indispensable ...but is it *more* valuable to you than paying down that depressing debt?

When you use your deepest values as your yardstick, these choices become easier. It may feel miserable to trim down your food or eating budget, but it may energize you to make those same cuts if you know that the money you're saving is going to wards buying a gift for someone you love, or for the holiday of a lifetime, or your child's education. The great thing about editing your budget according to *your own values* is that you're not making or saving more money, but using the money you already have to its best purpose. You're optimizing. And so you don't have to feel miserable forcing yourself to be frugal, because your actions are naturally geared towards a lifestyle that means something to you. You're not trimming your budget, you're enriching your life. You're not taking away, but *adding*.

Step four - Develop active habits:

All the money epiphanies in the world mean nothing until they're put into action. The whole point of looking closely at your spending habits, your money psychology and the misconceptions fuelling your spending habits is simple: *do* something about it.

Thankfully, the smallest changes are sometimes the best. Don't worry about making grand one-time gestures to fix up your money troubles once and for all. Rather, focus on small, realistic habits that you can do each and every day. It's these changes, after all, that will accumulate and go to making up the bulk of the life you want to create.

Let's say you commit to dropping expensive dinners with your partner. Many of us just default to eating as entertainment – but there's so much more to life than eating! Instead spend that money on things that you both actually enjoy: buy board games, save up for a hobby you can both do together or go to interesting talks or workshops. Instead of taking public transport, take your bike and you save money and get some fitness into your schedule at the same time.

Here's a more extreme example. Let's say you look at your budget and realize that although you deeply value travelling and learning about new and exciting places, you haven't actually been able to afford a real holiday for years. But you fritter away money every year on travelling to visit distant family members, people who you don't like much and who don't seem to like you either. Not only do these family members add nothing to your life, they actively make you less happy by adding stress and keeping you from putting that money towards a trip that would actually make you happy.

Just by looking realistically at your budget, you've discovered that you have also been spending too much time on unfulfilling relationships that are more about obligation than anything else. Without spending an extra cent, you make it a habit to treat yourself each year to a weekly vacation somewhere *you* want to go.

Step five - Rinse and repeat:

As we've seen, happy spending habits are more or less always a work in progress. Make daily changes to your life and try on new habits for size. Then have another look and ask how those changes are working for you. Can you change something else? Is there something new you've learnt? Have you learnt how *not* to do it?

Tips on Surviving a Money Crazy World:

Avoid, wherever you can, the temptation to spend on impulse. If you always give yourself a "cooling off period," you'll minimize emotional spending or buying something just because of sneaky advertising. For smaller purchases, wait 24 hours, and for bigger purchases, sleep on it for a few days before committing.

When you're spending money on something, don't focus only on the price you see in front of you. Ask yourself what this item *really costs you*. How long did you have to work to afford it? By working that long and exchanging that time for money for this item, did you really get a "good deal"? Could you use that time or that money on something else, that's worth more to you? Is that money actually worth more *unspent*, i.e. do you really have to buy anything at all?

Fast forward purchases a few years. Many of us throw away huge amounts of junk from our homes every year, and also keep buying things obsessively, never making the connection between the two. Are you going to get bored of this item within a few months? Will it really last? How will it fit into your life? Are you actually just buying next year's junk?

Don't go to shopping malls unless you're feeling calm, rational and in control. This means avoiding the shops when you're hungry, sad, bored, angry... You'll only be extra susceptible to advertising and pressure to "buy solutions." You'll have to work extra hard to resist temptation and may fall into the trap of feeling that you're depriving yourself.

Be prepared. It's so much easier to act wisely when you're acting according to a plan you've spent time on beforehand. Know how much you can afford to spend on a night out before you leave. Go shopping with a list and don't buy anything not on that list. Pack a work lunch the night before so you're not tempted to buy something expensive on the spur of the moment when you get hungry.

Try to see if you can spend your money on lived experiences rather than things. Things get old. They break. People get bored of them. But happy memories can last a lifetime, and if your experience teaches you a new skill or gives you a fresh insight on life, even better. Think of travelling somewhere novel, seeing a show, going to a class to learn something new, challenging yourself to a marathon or climb, donating to a charity that means something to you, experiencing beautiful music or performances, going into nature ...all of these things have so much more value compared to something like a phone upgrade or a new piece of furniture for your home.

Carry only small amounts of cash on you, for emergencies. This will deter you from spending mindlessly. It's easy to think of a few coins in your wallet as nothing much, but they add up. Spending on bank cards has the added advantage of letting you track exactly how much and on what you spend your money.

If you're trying to develop your professional career, you might like to consider negotiating for and working towards a higher hourly rate with less total time worked rather than endlessly angling for more work. In the long term, you'll value your *time* more and more. As you upskill and become more experienced, look for more job flexibility, more benefits and more free time rather than just a higher salary. Employers are usually a bit happier to negotiate on these anyway, and they'll actually have a greater impact on your quality of life.

When making big spending decisions, consider how a choice will mature with time. It may be that it's better to spend on X rather than Y in the present moment, but wait ten years and X just gets worse and worse as a choice. When considering big purchases, spending on education or paying off debt, ask yourself what will give you the greatest flexibility and control in the future. Ask which choice gives you more choices later on. Give less weight to choices that can't be undone or modified and more weight to those that can.

Don't be afraid to talk about money. Let go of hang ups and ask for help and advice when you need it. There's no shame in having money difficulties or being stuck with debt – but it's a real shame if you let hang ups about money prevent you from tackling a serious problem head on.

Some of our most nonsensical spending habits are closely tied with our worst life habits in general. Do you have an unhealthy drinking or smoking habit? This is the kind of thing you pay for over and over again – you pay for the substance itself, you pay with diminished health and you may even have to pay later on for medicine or treatment for health problems you bring on yourself. When it comes to any kind of addiction, it's never worth it. If this is you, the best thing you can do for yourself is clean up this bad habit. Drop your nasty sugar addiction. Quit smoking. Cut back on drinking. Vow to stay away from junk food.

Speaking of habits, there's one that you can get rid of instantly: gambling. If you're throwing away money on casinos or lottery tickets (or, as my grandmother called it, "idiot tax") then just stop. That money will do far more for you as savings.

Avoid comparing yourself to others. There's a lot of ego bound up in money, and it's hard to break the automatic connection that money = success. If you're suffering from trying to keep up with your peers, try to remember that people willfully display the life they want you to see, and there are invariably problems that you never know about. Keep going towards your own goals. If someone's success feels intimidating, try turn that feeling into inspiration – how can you do the same? What can you learn from them?

Conclusion

At the beginning of this book, I asked you to answer the question, "what is money?"

Well, let's look again at this question as we come to the end of the book. Do you still have the same definition of money? Or have you altered it slightly, or made it a little larger?

The way you think about money is highly personal – your attitude to money is a reflection of your upbringing, your culture, your personality with all its virtues and shortcomings. Money can be a literal prison, tying you down to work and habits that drain you of motivation and purpose. It can also be a bridge that carries you to your life goals, a tool and a resource that allows you to access the things you truly value in life.

The role that money ultimately plays in your life is entirely up to you. It rests in having the self awareness to be honest about the choices we make every day, in the bravery to know what we value and hold dear, and the dedication to make rational strategies to reach those goals.

My hope is that this book has given you a starting point to begin to reconsider your relationship to money and, by extension, your relationship to yourself and the world you live in. My hope is that you've found something here that inspires you to think differently and make different choices, ones that will leave you feeling more in control and more fulfilled than before. We each only have one life – here's to spending it wisely!

*****

Bonus previews

"The Minimalist Budget: A Practical Guide On How To Save Money, Spend Less And Live More With A Minimalist Lifestyle"

What's the first thing you think of when you hear the word "budget"? It's a meager little word, one that all too often comes after "tight". Maybe you think of this word as an adjective, something to describe a cheap and substandard car or hotel. "Budget" brings to mind rationing, a kind of money diet. If you're like many people, budgeting is something you do with a kind of deflated spirit: budgeting means bargain bin quality and the sad sense that what you want is going to be just out of reach.

This book will try a different approach to budgeting all together. It's a pity that the idea of living within one's means should be experienced as such a deficit – this book will try to show that when you apply the principles of minimalism to budgeting, you are neither in a state of self-denial or trying to survive a financial scrape. In fact, a minimalist budget is a particular approach to abundance and fulfillment that may seem counterintuitive to most.

Undoubtedly, what came into your mind when you heard the word "budget" was simple: money. Money is a thing to be feared, to be saved, to be celebrated when it's there and mourned when it isn't. Budgeting, we are told, is necessary. When you live in a world where there is always one more thing to buy, being cognizant of the fact that you don't have endless resources is just the practical thing to do.

However, budgeting can be much more than this. To put it simply, money is only *one* of the resources that we should be managing in our lives, and possibly not even the most important one.

As humans, it is our lot to deal with being finite beings: we have only so much time to spend on this earth, only so much time that we are allotted each day, only so much energy that we can give away before we run into a deficit.

In a sense, the principles of minimalism rest on a more fundamental interpretation of "budget". Just as you need to match your financial expenditure with your income, minimalism encourages us to match our needs with our actions. It doesn't make sense to buy food for 12 when you have a family of 4 in the same way it doesn't make sense to clutter up your home with things you don't want, like or need. Trimming away at unessential elements in your day-to-day life is an exercise in budgeting and minimalism both, whether you are trimming away excess expenses, destructive thoughts or junk in your spare room.

This book will offer an expanded notion of what it means to budget. We'll look at how money is not the only resource that needs to be managed, and a "life budget" that acknowledges your emotional, behavioral, social and even spiritual capital is more likely to lead to smarter decisions.

Minimalism is not, of course, about starvation or punishment. It's not about doing with less than you need. Rather, minimalism is about finding what you need and fulfilling that need exactly, without excess. It's a subtle point and one that the average person who has grown up in an industrialized capitalist society can miss: *to have exactly enough is not suffering*. Budgeting is therefore about understanding what you need to have enough, and how best you can allocate your resources to that end.

Most of the budgeting advice out there will come firmly out of the scarcity paradigm – you're usually offered a few ways to shave off money here and there. You are asked to look at all the instances where you are not spending or living on the bare minimum, and usually anything extra is framed as unnecessary, indulgent or, depending on who you talk to, bordering on immoral. These tips will tell you that after enough cheap toothpaste, homemade laundry soap and clothes bought out of season, you'll save enough money and make it all work. You're asked to look over your life and find places where you could manage, without too much discomfort, to do with less or even without.

While thriftiness and being money-conscious are excellent skills to have (and for some, absolutely necessary), minimalist budgeting is more about conscious decision making and less about stinginess and trying to endure a lack.

To show the difference, consider a purchase someone might make: a new dishwasher. On paper, the initial cost of a dishwasher might make it look like a kind of luxury. After all, you can simply wash the dishes *for free* yourself, right? In traditional budget land, a dishwasher may fall well into the category of "unnecessary". Can you do without it? Of course. Then, it doesn't belong in your pared down budget. On the face of it, this logic seems sound. In fact, while you're laboring away washing dishes by hand, you may even get the impression that doing it all yourself is kind of noble.

The "minimalist budgeting" in this book will ask you to take a more expanded view of the dishwasher. Not buying one will certainly result in less of your money spent. But, as mentioned, since money is not your only resource, by focusing on only this aspect you're not getting the full picture. Is the cost of doing dishes by hand *really* free? In your budget, have you factored in the fact that washing dishes saps hours of your life each week and makes you grumpy? If you're so wiped out at the prospect of another 45 minutes of housework at the end of the day that you give up and splash out on expensive restaurant food, you haven't even saved money, anyway.

When you lay alone in bed at night and ponder your existence, which will mean more to you: the extra cash you saved by not buying a dishwasher, or the lifestyle you gave up as the person who never has to worry about dishes again? You can't take your possessions with you when you die, they say, but which will be more soothing to you on your deathbed - the fact that your life was thrifty or that it was enjoyable and meaningful?

Simple budgeting doesn't take these kinds of things into account. The primary purpose of your life, at least in some sense, is to be happy. Money usually facilitates this. But if you're maximizing your money to the point that it makes you less happy, your budget is no longer serving its purpose. Minimalist budgeting is like regular budgeting, only with an eye to what is truly important. While this book will certainly show you nifty ways to save a buck here and there, it will also regularly ask you to examine what that buck means to you at the end of the day.

We'll explore shopping and spending habits, identify problem areas, think about debt and make achievable goals for home, work and more. We'll look at concrete ways to put some of these principles into action, and look at resources that will keep you focused and motivated. But at the same time, this book is also about the philosophy of minimalism, not thriftiness. If you can pair your budget plan with a more nuanced understanding of your relationship with money and how it ties into how you want to live, the changes you make will be more authentic and longer lasting.

"Self-Compassion - I Don't Have To Feel Better Than Others To Feel Good About Myself: Learn How To See Self Esteem Through The Lens Of Self-Love and Mindfulness and Cultivate The Courage To Be You"

The world is a vast, complicated and sometimes downright hostile place. Today, more than ever, human beings have had to learn new ways to be resilient, know themselves and have the courage to be who they are. Our hyper connected world bombards us with images of phenomenally successful celebrities together with the expectation that we should want nothing but the best for ourselves at all times. But in a bustling world of 7 billion people, carving out a meaningful niche for ourselves can be daunting to say the least.

It's understandable that people feel the need to bolster their self esteem. Faced with millions of glossy images in the media about how we should live our lives, some have turned to trying even harder still to keep up. Others have merely given up. It's no exaggeration that people in the 21st century live in a world of infinitely more possibilities than any generation before them. We have experts and gurus of all stripes telling us that the life we have now is nothing compared to what we could achieve – and yet, we're as depressed and lacking in confidence as ever.

Self help books on the market today will tell you one of two things: either that you are perfect already as you are and needn't worry, or that with just a little (well, a lot) of effort, you *can* reach those goals. Be the best, smartest, most successful, thinnest and relentlessly happiest version of yourself possible. No excuses!

This book takes a different approach to self esteem altogether. If you're feeling overwhelmed and worthless, inundated with information, struggling to juggle life, expectations, and disappointments... it may be time for a little self-compassion.

Unlike self esteem or an inflated confidence level, self-compassion is a different way of looking at yourself and others, warts and all, and a way more realistic acceptance of the way things are. With self-compassion, you become unflappable, calm and self-assured - without the risk of narcissism or becoming self-absorbed. Through a series of exercises, this book will suggest a new, gentle yet extremely powerful attitude shift that can end feelings of self-hatred, doubt, shame and low self-worth forever.

"How To Stop Worrying and Start Living - What Other People Think Of Me Is None Of My Business"

Stress is a lot like love – hard to define, but you know it when you feel it.

This book will explore the nature of stress and how it infiltrates every level of your life, including the physical, emotional, cognitive, relational and even spiritual. You'll find ways to nurture resilience, rationality and relaxation in your every day life, and learn how to loosen the grip of worry and anxiety. Through techniques that get to the heart of your unique stress response, and an exploration of how stress can affect your relationships, you'll discover how to control stress instead of letting it control you. This book shows you how.

But this book is not just another "anti-stress" book. Here, we will not be concerned with only reducing the symptoms of stress. Rather, we'll try to understand exactly what stress is and the role it plays in our lives. We'll attempt to dig deep to really understand the real sources of our anxiety and how to take ownership of them. Using the power of habit and several techniques for smoothing out the stressful wrinkles in our day-to-day lives, we'll move towards a real-world solution to living with less stress, more confidence and a deep spiritual resilience that will insulate you from the inevitable pressures of life.

By adopting a trusting, open and relaxed attitude, we'll bring something more of ourselves to relationships of all kinds. This book will take a look at dating and relationships without stress and worry, as well as ways to bring tranquility and balance into your home and family life. Again, this book is not about eradicating stress from your life forever. We'll end with a consideration of the positive side of negative thinking, and how we can use stress and worry to our advantage.

We will address physical, emotional, relational, spiritual, and cognitive and behavioral symptoms of stress.

And while most stress-management solutions offer relief for symptoms in only one or two of the above areas, this book will show you how all five areas are important, and a successful stress solution will touch on each of them.

"Codependency - "Loves Me, Loves Me Not": Learn How To Cultivate Healthy Relationships, Overcome Relationship Jealousy, Stop Controlling Others and Be Codependent No More"

If you've had difficulty with starting or maintaining relationships, issues with feeling jealous and possessive or find that your connections with others are more a source of distress than anything else, this book is for you.

By finding ways to be more mindful throughout the day, as well as exercises in improving your communication skills, this book will show you how to have relationships that are calmer and more stable and compassionate.

We'll begin with a look at the phenomenon of codependency, what it has traditionally meant in the psychological realm and how these traits and patterns can be traced back to issues of self-worth, compassion and more deliberate action. We'll examine how mindfulness can be the magic ingredient to getting a hold of the codependency cycle, and some of the characteristics of happy, mindful relationships. Finally, we'll explore a model for mindful communication and ways that you can begin to implement immediately in order to make a commitment to stronger, more compassionate relationships with others.

It may feel sometimes that an intense and serious connection with someone is proof of the depth of the feeling you have for one another. But be careful, obsession and dependency is not the same as love. In the codependent relationship, our affection and attention is coming from a place of fear and need. As a result, the partners never really connect with each other. They do endless, complicated dances around each others problems, but what they never do is make an honest human connection.

In codependent relationships, manipulation, guilt and resentment take the place of healthy, balanced affection. Codependent partners are not necessarily together because they want to be, they are because they have to be, because they don't know how to live otherwise. One partner may bring a history of abuse, a "personality disorder" or mental illness into a relationship; the ways the other partner responds to this may be healthy or not, but if they bring their own issues to the table too, they may find that the bond of their love is more accurately described as a shared and complementary dysfunction.

Remember, the relationships we are in can never be better than the relationships we have with ourselves. Two unhappy people together never make a happy couple together. We cannot treat other people in ways we have never taken the time to consider before, and we cannot communicate properly if we are not even sure what it is we need to communicate in the first place.

An individual with a mature, well-developed sense of themselves has the most to offer someone else. They have their own lives, their own sense of self-worth, their own strength. And when you remove need, fear, obsession and desperation, you open up the way for love and affection just for its own sake.

Love is many things, but it's cheapened when held hostage by the ego. Connections formed around ego and fear may be strong and lasting, but what keeps them going is mutual need. What could be more romantic than, "I don't need to be with you. You don't complete me at all. I am happy and stable and fulfilled without you. But I still want to be with you, because you're awesome"?

On the ground, in the nitty gritty of life, we can reduce a massive thing like "Relationships" down to smaller, more manageable units. Everything from the deepest and most profound romantic and spiritual union to sharing a joke with the cashier at the supermarket rests on one thing: communication. Whether it's through words or not, we are constantly communicating, and the accumulation of these little units creates this big thing we call a relationship.

"Love Is A Verb - 30 Days To Improving Your Relationship Communication: Learn How To Nurture A Deeper Love By Mastering The Art of Heart-To-Heart Relationship Communication"

Have you ever noticed how often people say they wish they could "find" love? As if love were something beautiful to just stumble upon on the side of the road. Yet when you speak to happily married couples, especially those that have been married for decades, they never ascribe their success and happiness to luck. Instead, they'll probably tell you that a good relationship takes work - lots of it - and the continued effort and maintenance from both sides.

Love is a *verb*.

It is not something only some people are fortunate enough to catch and then merely set aside. It's not a prize you win or a box to tick on your life's checklist. Instead, love has to be kindled and rebuilt *every day*; it has to be invited in, nurtured, cultivated. Love is not something passive that you simply have or don't have - it's an active process and the continual expression of what's in your heart, mind and soul.

In this book, love is not a noun. It isn't some mysterious gift from the gods that falls into our laps, but something that we can work on and build with intention. So, in that spirit, this book will not be a dispassionate list of relationship advice, or theories about the way people work together, or tips to heat up your sex life.

Instead, this book will ask you to become *actively* involved, to not just read but to constantly apply what has been read to your own life. And since we are on the topic of heart-to-heart communication, you're naturally going to need to rope in your partner, too. The exercises are experiential, meaning, simply, that you have to actually *do* them in order to benefit from them.

You'll be asked to be honest with yourself, get out there into the world and even make yourself vulnerable. Some of these exercises will ﹏n, others will scare and challenge you - but they are all designed pen your heart to more effective communication with others, so that the relationships you build are strong, heart centered and compassionate.

This book is written for anyone who feels that they are not living (and loving!) to their full potential. Whether you crave deeper connections with others or want to reignite relationships you are already in, this book was written to help you master the art of good communication.

In fact, it would be ideal for you to think of this book itself as one of the first of many new and interesting conversations you're going to have. Although I don't know you and cannot be sure of your response to what's written in these pages, I want for to engage with and respond to everything here as though I was sitting right there in the room with you.

You don't have to agree with everything, or like the principles outlined here. The important thing, though, is that in opening up the dialogue, you are already taking those first few steps to becoming more conscious, compassionate lovers and partners.

When we risk nothing, we gain nothing. When we don't open ourselves to love, we don't love deeply. My wish is that this book leaves you feeling open and receptive to love - your own ability to give it as well as the privilege of receiving it. And I hope that you have high expectations for yourself in reading it, too.

When two people come together, in any capacity, there is the chance for something special to happen. Every great romance began with a meeting of two hearts, with the first word of the first conversation. Let's begin this book with the first word. I am pleased to meet you, dear reader, and hope that in moving through this book together, we can jointly create a little more love, a little more tenderness and a little more understanding in the world than there was to begin with.

"Mindful Eating: A Healthy, Balanced and Compassionate Way To Stop Overeating, How To Lose Weight and Get a Real Taste of Life by Eating Mindfully"

What are you hungry for?

You may have been drawn to the idea of mindful eating as an antidote to the empty promises of the diet industry, or you may have felt that it's time to pursue a more purposeful, more compassionate way of eating. Whatever your reasons and whatever your current relationship to food and your body is, this book can help you reconsider your eating habits and whether they are truly serving your highest good.

Through an exploration of the real reasons we overeat, our thoughts and feelings around food, and coming into closer contact with our own true appetites, this book aims to help you craft an open and accepting attitude towards food.

Mindful eating is an attitude towards food (and much more) that encourages awareness, deliberate action and an open acceptance of the present moment as it unfolds around us.

In this book, we'll look at how the conventional dieting mindset is actually damaging and counterproductive, and how mindful eating can be a refreshing break away from all the expectations that you have about yourself and food that are not serving you. The ultimate goal is to become exquisitely tuned in to your own appetites, desires and passions, and to tune out the noise and clutter from the outside world that muffle your innate intuition about what is good for you and what isn't.

When we understand our true hunger, when we realize the psychological, emotional, behavioral, physical and even spiritual causes behind our overeating, only then can we can start to take realistic steps to remedy it.

"Minimalism: How To Declutter, De-Stress And Simplify Your Life With Simple Living"

Today, a growing number of people are becoming dissatisfied with their lives and turning to simpler ways of working, living and raising their children.

This book will explore the philosophy of minimalism and how it can streamline your life, declutter your home, reduce stress, mindless consumerism, and reconnect you to what's truly important.

You'll find ways to adopt a mindset that promotes simplicity and elegance in your every day life, and rethink your dependence on material possessions. We will explore how practical changes to our surroundings can lead to a previously unknown inner peace and calm. Whether in our wardrobes, kitchens, work lives or our deeper sense of personal and spiritual purpose, we could all do with focusing on things that align with our values and reducing the distraction of those things that pull us away from them. This book shows you how.

For those born and raised in the height of our consumer society, the idea that happiness and personal fulfillment is found in stuff is more or less a given. The capitalist machine we all live within requires only one thing of us: that we should constantly want, and the things we should want are to be found, usually, in malls. Malls that are filled with strategically placed advertising, with the sole purpose to entice and lure you, trying to convince you that you need, not want, their specific product. Our economy relies heavily on a steady stream of consumption: better clothes, cars, bigger houses and things to fill those houses with, the newest appliances, Christmas decorations, pet toys, jewelry, office furniture, pot plants, gaming consoles, specialty tires, luxury soaps... the array of stuff is simply dazzling.

But if you are reading this there's a chance you find this overabundance just a little... exhausting. Paradoxically, there seems to be a sad sort of emptiness in filling up one's life with more things. What is simple and truly valuable often seems to be completely hidden under mountains of what is unnecessary. Although advertising tells us the best way to solve problems is to buy solutions, tranquility and a graceful life seem to elude us, no matter what we buy or how much of it.

Minimalism is an aesthetic, a philosophy and a way of life. This book takes a look at how deeply liberating a simpler life can be, and shows you ways you can adopt a calmer, more deliberate way of living and working. Minimalism is about clearing away the clutter that is distracting from what is really important. It's about rethinking our attitudes to ownership, to our lifestyles and to our innermost values.

"Creative Writing - From Think To Ink: Learn How To Unleash Your Creative Self and Discover Why You Don't Need 1000 Writing Prompts To Blast Away Your Writer's Block and Improve Your Writing Skills"

Plenty of writing advice out there is focused on the nuts and bolts of writing – how to do it, when, how to market it and where, etc. But this is not that sort of book. If you want to learn to write more compellingly, with more skill and expertise, you can do it, easily. The really tricky bit, though, is understanding why.

Uncover this why for yourself and you get in touch with the inexhaustible engine of your creativity. The human core of why we bother to create at all. Get to know this root well and you will not need gimmicky books full of writing prompts to blast away your writer's block. You will not need "inspiration" or 31 awesome tips and tricks. When you were a baby, something made you open your mouth and speak. Understand the thing that inspired you to do this, and you're more than half way to being the creative, productive and generative human being you were destined to be.

When you were a tiny baby, your head was full of mostly nothing and the world was new and unknown. You barely had the skill to move yourself around the environment, and you most definitely lacked the skill to do what humans are most know for – communication.

As you grew and developed, though, something strange started to happen. The people around you, the things in your world - you began to understand that they could be reached. That in your infant isolation there was still a way to reach out and touch someone else's experience. You saw all around you evidence of this magical skill that you had yet to develop: language.

Since before we were old enough to understand it, we've tried to master this almost god-like ability to shape symbols and concepts, reach into the mind of someone else and affect their hearts and minds, to bring about changes in the world, to connect and understand and share with another human being.

At the root of all creative expression is a deep, inborn and very human desire to be heard and understood.

For the writers among us, the urge to communicate more clearly, more beautifully, and in new ways never really left us. With the right words, new worlds can be created, new ideas can be incubated and grown, great heights and depths can be reached. Every brilliant idea had its first home in the written or spoken word, and if you are a writer or aspire to be one, you most likely understand this power better than anything.

Ask yourself this simple question: why write at all?

Once you've managed to answer this question for yourself you'll have found something that will be incredibly valuable to your writing career, wherever it takes you: your purpose.

Tapping into the deep roots of why you are compelled to write at all is a brilliant way to unlock your true motivations and your ultimate reason for that urge to take what's in your head and put it out there in the world.

Remember, all change and growth begins with the creativity of imagining something different. It's quite likely that opening the door on your innate creativity will invite all sorts of new skills and insights into your life, not just the verbal ones.

87326684R00028

Made in the USA
Columbia, SC
12 January 2018